Ask the Family

If you are collecting your family history, the first source must always be the family itself. You could, it is true, start knowing just your own name and date of birth, and work back through official records, but this is not only a very expensive way of going about things, but also a very chilly business, lacking the warmth and humour of family life, which turns clinical genealogy into living family history. Unless you are a complete orphan, you will be able to collect some of that precious personal knowledge for yourself.

When to Start

Now. Even if you are too young to travel around gathering information from official repositories, or too tied to the house to spend much time on the work now, grab any possible opportunity. Talk to the older generation in the family and take careful note of what they have to tell you. Even if you can't make use of it now, store it up against the time when you have better chances to carry on the search. If you postpone starting until you have time, all the old folk may be dead and the rest not speaking to you becuase you never bothered with them before.

Who to Ask

Anybody who is older than you (or anybody who has been in close contact with members of the family older than you. And don't be put off by those who say "It's no use asking Aunt Fanny – she doesn't remember what she had for breakfast, poor dear". That may well be true, but if your breakfast was boring plastic slop, you would want to forget it too. If you get her talking about the days when she was young and happy, you may find she has total recall of everything and everyone. Often, elderly people have ceased to communicate because no one will bother to communicate with them. Spend a little time with them and they will open up again. You may think that old people only talk about boring things like bingo and bowls. They think that young people only talk about boring things like pop records and football. True?

You will have to be prepared for a certain amount of problems at the beginning, and for some time being wasted on things you are not interested in or opinions you don't agree with. That applies to most television programmes, evenings out at the pub or dinner with the boss. It is up to you to steer the conversation round to more interesting channels – or listen with an open mind and maybe get interested.

Who to Start On

Obviously, if Great Aunt Fanny is over 90 and in frail health, you must approach her pretty soon. However, it is best, if you can, to practise your technique nearer home first, with Mum or sister Sally. Then if you get confused or start asking questions in a way that upsets them, you will know enough to do better when you see Auntie. It helps, too, if you have collected the more obvious stuff about the later generations of the family, and can start with some sort of pedigree in hand, rather than stopping Auntie every few minutes to spell or repeat a name. If you keep stumbling, or react with surprise to some well-known (to her) bit of family history, you are going to throw the old lady and maybe stop the flow. Cut your teeth on your nearest and dearest and try to get the background clear in your own mind. But if you hear that the end is nigh, don't fail to go because you think you will make a mess of it. Better a mess than nothing at all. You might even give the old lady a new lease of life, because someone is interested at last.

Why not just write – or phone?

Distant relatives are best interviewed rather than written to, if this is at all practical. Why not go to Mudflat to see Auntie Maggie instead of joining the traffic jam to the coast next Bank Holiday ? Some elderly people are not very good at reading or writing, either through lack of formal education or through failing sight or arthritic hands. Others just can't be bothered to put pen to paper, or don't see why they should, or write but forget to post the letter. In most cases, if only you went, you would get the answer you want. Even people who write are not usually as gloriously indiscreet on paper as they would be face to face. They won't commit to paper their opinion of Cousin Jane, in case she sees the letter, neither will they speculate about the parentage of Lizzie's baby – after all, you are a stranger and you might be shocked.

By all means write first to explain who you are and what you want, but try to follow it up with a personal visit if you possibly can. You could try phoning, but remember that some old people are rather scared of the phone, others don't talk freely into the air, never knowing who is listening, and many more are rather deaf and find it a strain to listen for long.

If you don't get an answer, this could be because of the mechanical problems when writing mentioned above; or because stamps cost money (and you forgot to include an S.A.E.); or because that nice Mrs Brown offered to post the letter and forgot; or because they have lost the letter or forgotten it. After a decent interval, write again saying you are coming down next Wednesday and will call, but if it is not convenient, then how about Wednesday week, or would they suggest a day ? This may get action, but if not, go on Wednesday – they can't say they haven't been warned. Don't just drop in – it embarrasses people to be caught in the middle of a mess, or without a biscuit in the house. An exception to that is if the old relative is a known recluse, given to locking the door and hiding. Then arrive (plus biscuits) and get your foot in the door – having made a noise like a milk bottle to get him to open up.

Prepare to meet thy doom

Time – set aside the whole day for the visit if necessary. You will get nowhere if you try to do the interview in a rush on the way to somewhere else. Don't keep looking at your watch – you have the rest of your life to play with – Auntie may only have a few months left.

Dress – carefully. If you go dripping mink, then you are a snob and would not possibly want to know the sordid truth about Uncle Charlie. Don't go to the other extreme and wear your scruffy jeans – you are after the spoons, letting down the side, shaming her before the neighbours. Trousers at all on females upset some old folk. High fashion of any kind, especially on men, is worrying and Punk hair cuts irritate. You want something from Auntie, so make every concession to her susceptibilities. Nice, neat, conservative garments, no extremes of any kind. Park the Rolls where it will impress the neighbours but Auntie will only spot it after you have established yourself and been classed as a nice, friendly body, with no airs.

Children – not recommended under about twelve at all. The sweetest little angels turn into fiends when they are visiting. They resent not being the centre of attention, or, if they are, it distracts from the purpose of the visit. The cakes they stuff down them will return dramatically half way back up the motorway. Even sensible children behaving normally find problems in adapting their movements to a house not geared to the young. They knock over the Dresden shepherdess or break the handles off bone china or terrify the cat and budgie. If you must take the family, show them off all prettied up for five minutes, then send them off with a minder for the rest of the day (and a change of clothes). Let them back for the last fifteen minutes of the visit, mopped and subdued, then get rid of them before they start making remarks about uncle's red nose or the funny smell.

Photos of children are something else again. They may spark off an extra reminiscence about our Jimmie who used to look just like that before he was took.

Spouses and teenagers above the clodhoppy stage. They can be very useful, if they will sit tight and make the right noises. If they will look after the tape recorder (see page 8) or can take good photos, they are valuable indeed. But the sort of man who yatters on about his car and his importance and what he would say to the Unions if, or the woman who sits there like a Christian martyr, resenting every mention of the family, or the young horror who whines about being home in time for the disco are best left at home, or sent out as minders with the younger ones, or quietly pushed under a bus.

Dogs – preferably not. They are worse than children for knocking things down; they chase the cats; they dig up the flower bed; they bump into auntie when she is carrying the tea tray. Even doggy households like their own dogs, not yours.

Cats – the native cat is sacred. Don't sit on her chair or brush her off your lap. Wear clothes which will stand being clawed or haired on and bite back the scream if you are bitten ("Tibby's got a bad ear, dear.").

Food – eat and drink whatever is put before you, with great enthusiasm but reasonable moderation.   If you are actively allergic, say how much you love it but the wicked doctor has forbidden it. Otherwise, eat what comes and throw up later. You might even like it. If you are worried about the expense of the amount the family have eaten, then take along milk and bread (just happen to have it in the car) and some edible gift.   If the amount provided is very considerable and obviously beyond their means, don't offer money.   That is an insult.   Send a replacement soon after – not precisely the same (ours isn't good enough) but similar (because you really know what good food is).

Smell – sometimes, old people's houses smell odd.   Ventilation is a draught to them.   Sometimes people smell odd.   It isn't easy when you are frail and arthritic to keep yourself or your house spotless – besides, who ever comes round to see. So when you go in, don't sniff the air and ask for the windows to be opened.   And don't stare round the room.   You are there to talk, not to do a housing inspection. And, if the house is neat and clean, don't smoke cigarettes unless pressed.   It takes weeks to get the stink out of covers and corners. Smoke can be actively distressing to someone with respiratory trouble.

Timing – old people may flag after talking for an hour or so (or they may go on until you are dropping in your tracks).   If your interviewee shows the slightest sign of distress, let up for a while. She may recover after half an hour's nap, or that may be it for the day. So you are disappointed because you have come 85 miles. Auntie has come 85 years – how do you think she feels? You can surely come back again another day.   Don't try to force more out of the old lady than she can give that day, or that will be the last chance you get to see her.   Leave the house with the feeling that you can come back again and welcome (and don't wait too long).

Contacting distant relations

When you have exhausted the family you know well, there will come a stage when you start on those you haven't seen since you were six – or that your mother hasn't seen since *she* was six.   After that come the interviews with complete strangers.   Obviously, you will write first saying who you are and what you want.   Tracing family history is acceptable as a form of madness nowadays, and establishing yourself as the family's genealogy nut is no bad thing.

Your motives must be made crystal clear. If the relative has money there will naturally be the suspicion that you are after it.   If you discover that Aunt Maud is filthy rich, then do go in the mink bearing a single rose.   What is more difficult is the more normal case where Auntie has a very little nest egg, which was valuable once. She is liable to think you are after the spoons, or, if you go on about how much money you have and how little you need her spoons, she will think you despise her treasures.   Somehow, you have to spot an object which is attractive but by no means valuable and praise that. If you can convince Auntie that you rate the old tea caddy as highly as the spoons, then maybe you will get the lot one day. More important, you will get the story.

This is quite a difficult problem, for if you appear to scorn worldly goods, someone else will get what you covet as a memento of your ancestors. Somehow, you have to persuade the family that you are a suitable custodian for anything "family", however trivial – or valuable, while getting it over that you are not "after something" at the outset.

You will be going into someone else's house and asking very personal questions. Can you persuade them that you are not a snooper from the Social Security in disguise? An elderly lady may not, anyway, like someone younger knowing all about her age and goings on. You will have to persuade her that you are not just nosey – that you want to share her knowledge of the family and that you will understand her problems. This means establishing yourself, not as a great-great-niece, too young to be told all the naughty bits, but more as a sort of worldly wise cousin, able to comprehend and enjoy all that is confided, without making moral judgements. It is quite possible to bridge the generation gap. People are people first, and age groups long after, so think yourself on to the same wavelength as your informant, and react as you would to a friend of your own age.

Cousin Flo. Very often, your aged person will be in the care of a middle-aged daughter or son. If you turn up on the doorstep, ready to charm the birds off the trees, you may meet a lot of resentment from the person who has to cope, day in, day out, with all the vagaries of which the elderly are capable. You have the time to be patient, the money to bring gifts, the stamina to pander for a couple of hours. Flo has got to cope with the reaction, the excitement, the demands for foie gras every day of the week and far more service than she is getting already. If this is the effect you have on Auntie, for sure she "won't be well enough to see you" next time. Enlist Flo's help, flatter her, send her a little gift that she will really like, help with the washing up, understand her problems too. Try to leave a good impression on her, not just on Auntie. Remember that in the fullness of time, when Auntie is gathered to her makers, it is likely to be Flo who clears up those lovely family papers. She could burn them, or pass them on to you – which do you think will be likely ?

You too can be an angel for a day at a time.

The sticky start

Sometimes, your relative won't play. The first stage is to identify yourself, if possible, by talking to her about someone she knows ("I'm your brother George's daughter Jean's daughter Carol") or showing photos of someone she knew at the date when she knew them. If you have that sort of photo, maybe get an enlarged print – old eyes

find it difficult to see something half an inch high.   If you have
the family face yourself, then half the battle is won.   Seize on any
memory you, or your parents, have of visits to the relative long ago.

Sometimes relatives (old men especially) are coarse or rude, seem-
ing intent on annoying you. Don't rise to it. It could be that they
have not moved in polite circles for so long they have forgotten how.
It could be that you are being tested to see if you are a squeamish
townee, not fit to hear the truth about the family.   Old people are
entitled to be rude (about your weight, your nose, your lack of hair,
the size of your family, the make of your car) and when you are
ninety, you can take full advantage of this.   It is all right for a
female to answer back to a man, in a very teasing way, and for a male
to tease auntie, but don't cheek someone of the same sex.

Sometimes the interviewee just won't talk.   Sometimes they have
lost the habit of talking to people, sometimes because, perversely,
now he has someone to talk to, Uncle wants to show his power by not
doing so.   Mothers who have potty trained difficult infants can cope
best with this line.   Some people won't talk because they have something to hide, or because they think the family is too commonplace
for you want to hear about.   You have to sell yourself as broad-
minded but not immoral.   You know just how hard life was in the old
days and how people didn't have the easy ways out they have now.
This usually covers illegitimacy, desertion, drunkenness, thieving.

If false humility is the problem, make it clear you know Grandpa
was a labourer and that you are interested in when he started work
and who he worked for too.   In fact, if the relative is just intent
on being cagy about family facts, you can sometimes get him going by
asking about the old days in general – compare farming then with now,
ask him what it was like at school when he was a boy.   If you really
have to fight to get him talking, chatter on about your own family
and bring each topic round to "I bet you didn't go to school by bus"
or "Did you have a big Birthday party when you were small" – hung on
short statements about little Jason and young Emma. Use any universal
topic to drag the conversation round by the scruff of its neck from
now to then.

Don't get carried away and spend the whole of the time talking
about yourself and your family, even if encouraged. You are not there
to sell *your* importance, *your* brilliance, *your* wonderful children,
your useless husband, but to listen and gather information.   Once
Uncle gets going, don't stop the flow to argue with his opinions.
Does it matter if he is racist? – ask him who lived next door when
he was a boy – he probably hated them too.   If he talks football,
don't blind him with science about modern teams – get him back to the
first match he ever attended ("With his brother? Did his father go?
What about his uncles? What were their names?").

If it is evident that Auntie is being cagy because of the presence
of Cousin Flo, can you sell yourself as harmless enough to get Flo
to go out for a nice walk (or a nice drive with your spouse) while

you talk? The root of the trouble may be that Flo arrived too soon after the wedding, but mustn't be told, to protect her innocent spinsterhood, or her mother's moral superiority. Nods, becks and winks might convey that you have guessed, and get things flowing.

Smooth running

Once you have got the conversation going, by whatever means, the problem then is to keep it running smoothly, without jerks and stops. One of the most difficult things is being sure who Auntie is talking about at any one time.

It eases matters if you always refer to relatives in the terms in which she would think of them. Thus "Father" is her father, "Grandpa" her grandfather not yours. Establish quickly whether Grandpa is her father's father and Gramp her mother's, or *vice versa*. Johnnie is your father, John your uncle on the other side. Bill is a brother and Willie a cousin. If you really can't work it out, ask once, then remember. Aim to keep the discussion to one generation at a time – this saves changing gear in mid reminiscence from the 1940s to 1920s to Edwardian times. However, don't ruin a promising train of chat because you haven't finished the list of Great Uncle Ernest's dozen children. If you get the same story twice, either listen to see if new details come out or, if it can be managed discreetly, seize on something in the middle to use as a starting point for another story.

React to the stories as if they were new – a grievance of fifty years ago may still rankle and need sympathy. But don't treat the facts as quaint bygones, and don't judge past events by today's standards. There was not always access to contraception or hostels for battered wives, so don't tell Auntie she should have left the drunken brute early on, before the six children arrived.

Read up the background, of history (for dates) and social history. But don't get carried away by a passion for academic research. Don't get so excited by talking to a relic of the General Strike period that you demand an opinion on the socio-economic consequences of the Jarrow march – unless Uncle is an economic historian. But if you know a bit about the period under discussion, this stops your cries of wild surprise at the wages and prices. If you know what the norm was, you can concentrate much more on the reasons why one of your family varied from it. Learn some basic dates which can be used for reference (the two wars, the Strike, the Flu, the Abdication, etc.).

If your informant has been chattering away nineteen to the dozen and suddenly clams up or goes cagy, think back to what you said. Did you mention Uncle Charlie – so what did he do to flutter the dovecot? Have you been pushing for dates of the marriage in front of Cousin Flo ? If the latter, leave it – you can check at St. Catherine's. If there is going to be no other source, probe gently, make a joke of wicked Uncle Charlie (a bit of a lad) but if Auntie looks distressed instead of mischievous, stop there. And never make a joke of her own mother or Granny.

Above all, don't push the elderly relative beyond his or her physical or mental endurance. Some frail bodies can't sit up for long, some frail minds can't stay clear for long. Watch out for signs of faltering and leave your questions there.

Recording

If you possibly can, record the interview. You won't remember the exact words said, and these may become important years later, after Auntie has passed to her reward. There is a difference between "He was born in Richmond", "He came from Richmond" and "The family came from Richmond" (even before you start on *which* Richmond). If you try to write it all down, you will most likely fail, unless you are a proficient shorthand writer, and even then, all those hooks and squiggles are a bit daunting. What are you writing? Are you really from the Social Security after all? Why are you hunched over the book, not looking Auntie in the face? Besides, if you are copying, you are not comprehending and reacting to the information as it comes and asking the right questions about the discrepant bits.

If you can, take a tape recorder with you. If you know the person and the house, a reel to reel recorder will give you better quality – after all, this is likely to be a social document of some importance to the family, and potentially to some local or national historian. But if the person's reactions are doubtful, taking a tape recorder is a risk. Some may refuse to talk, some become stilted and edit out the naughty bits. Then there is the little problem of plugs. There are some very odd bits of electric wiring in some elderly people's houses, and it doesn't help the flow of an interview if you have to change a plug from three pin ring mains to those funny little round things they use in Coventry.

If the reactions or mains equipment are at all doubtful, take a good battery cassette recorder. You may want to conceal the instrument, which is no problem as long as you have a good omni-directional mike close to the speaker – old voices don't carry far. You could mask the mike with your handbag or a camera or pretend it is an inhaler and snuffle a bit.

Provide the longest tape available, in case the going is good, and – ideally – have a quiet assistant to change tapes if necessary. Meanwhile, as you listen, take just a few notes of the rough layout of the family, so that you can be totally clear if you need to ask questions, or to prompt the next round of reminiscence. This way, you can be an attentive audience while not losing a syllable. If you have to change the tape solo, then go to the loo and take the machine with you rather than stop Auntie in her tracks while you scrabble behind a chair.

Always label the cassette with the date and name, and remove it from the reach of any of the family with a habit of wiping old tapes for re-use.

Photos and Pedigrees

Take with you as many photographs of the family as you can, even if you don't know quite who they are. Showing around mystery pictures is the best way to get them identified. Each relative you visit will probably have some photos. Just possibly, they might lend them, but more probably, they would let you make a copy on the spot. If you have a camera with a good portrait attachment (and ideally, someone to do it, who can concentrate on making a good job of it while you are talking) this will add to the value of your visit considerably. There is nothing like a photo to jog the memory. Even if the face is not recognised, the clothing may be - "Our Jimmie had a sailor suit like that".

Old photos have embossed stamps of the firm's name and address, if they are commercial ones (later ones have inked stamps on the back). The place may be worth asking about ("Why was cousin Marge in Heckmondwike?" "For Jane's wedding to Herbert Oldroyd."). Even landscapes and views of stately homes are not to be ignored. Did Martha work at Dotheboys Hall? Is that the view from Uncle Fred's farm? Conventional postcards from resorts tell you which place the family went to for holidays. They may have messages on the back with family information too. Make a note of the non-portrait photos in the family album and use the information on them.

Take round a portfolio of family photos if you can. Always ask for identifications, even when you know, since this may start a reminiscence going. People don't necessarily always recognise photos of themselves, but they will of relatives. If you want to do the job properly, you can sepia-tone your modern copies of old photos - it looks more authentic and it's fun.

Whether you write out the whole family pedigree and show it to Auntie before you start is an arguable point. It will certainly help you to have a complete draft of all the information you know already. But will it impress Auntie, confuse her or make her feel redundant? If you know her well, you can judge. If not, perhaps make several pedigrees - one with complete information, in case you want to refer to it; one with year dates and only the direct line in detail; one very simple one showing your name and auntie's and the link between the two. When you have judged which is suitable, produce it, and keep the others under wraps.

There is a big risk with producing a complete looking pedigree. Even if Auntie has information which would correct some important error, she may not like to say - you've got it written down, it must be true, or she doesn't want to argue with a nice person like you. If any information is doubtful, leave it out, pencil it, and/or put a big question mark. Try to get a list of the family in order before showing her what Uncle Joe said. He could easily be wrong. By all means send her a copy of the pedigree afterwards, if she shows interest, but if she seems rather prim, do gloss over the awkward marriage to baptism dates, since she may show it to a nosey neighbour and be embarrassed by having the dread truth about Granny spread around the district.

What to ask them

You want names, dates, occupations, places first, then appearance, characters, habits, motives, odd sayings, etc. The first four you could at a pinch get from official sources, so if your interviewee is very frail, settle for the latter ones – which you will probably get nowhere else. But in normal circumstances, if you have worked back through the family, up the generations, you should be able to collect enough basic information to save you pounds on certificates.

Ask the informant about his or her own family – the brothers and sisters, in order of birth, their full names (since pet names sometimes bear no relation to the registered name), their lives as young persons. If a great deal of detail on one brother, including his marriage and current address, emerges, go along with this, but if you are able to prompt, keep the informant's mind on one time period – more detail will come out that way. Ask where the children went to school, what clothes they wore, what jobs around the house they did, whether one was the favourite (jealousy fifty years on is a powerful spur to memory). When you have exhausted the children, ask about the father and mother, then their brothers and sisters, then the grandparents. Try to get it clear which side of the family you are talking about, referring to each person in the terms in which they would be known to your informant (Aunt Mary's boy Joe is *her* Aunt Mary, not yours). Don't be surprised if an elderly person doesn't know the first name of his grandparents – children were not encouraged to be familiar. You may be lucky if you get the surname of the mother's father. And be wary – Grandpa Sutton may be the grandfather who lived in Sutton, though his name was Foljambe.

Getting dates is more awkward. Unless your family is uncommonly numerate, then remembering actual dates is a difficult business. If you ask Auntie for the year when her brother Jim was born, she will either fret about not remembering, spend hours trying or pull some arbitrary date out of the air to shut you up. Ask for date order instead – was Jim older, how many years older, was he at school when Mary was born, and so on. If you can get this sort of comparison between the various family members mentioned, and then get one fix on the date of one of them, you can work out the rest.

Use national, local or personal events as fixed points for dating the family. Establish whether something happened "before the War" (which war?), "after the Somme", "in Coronation Year" (whose?); the year Arsenal won the Cup or Midnight Sun won the Derby; just before they built the Cottage Hospital; when they had the pageant at the Hall; the year I left school, got married, had our Georgie; buried Fred. The more cross checks you get the better, then any mistakes will be cancelled out.

Most people remember the day and month of their own birthdays and those of their siblings and parents. The year may be hazier. Sometimes people can do age (even of long dead people had they lived until now) but not the simple sums which provide the years. Obviously, you must not accept everything you are told as correct, but if the date given matches the official entry in the indexes at St. Catherine's House, then it is probably right. If the year is wrong, perhaps the day and month are correct, and you will find the entry in the corresponding quarter for the year before or after. Death dates are more likely to be wrong than births or marriages. Try to get a double fix on these – both "before the last war" and "while I was still at school". (People do remember the age and even the day when they left shcool, especially if they were poor scholars.)

You can check all national events in books or newspapers, and local ones in the latter source or a local history book. Don't stop the flow of the narrative to get out your little notebook and verify the date on the spot. It obviously helps if you carry at least some dates in your head – the two Wars for a start – so that you can tell if there is some major discrepancy between "Grandpa died in the Flu," (i.e., 1919) and "I was only a baby then" when she must have been at least twenty in 1919 by other evidence.

Locations. Some people can recall a whole lot of addresses where the family once lived, some have only vague notions of the town or even the house (red brick, on the corner).   Anything may help which gives a notion of where the family lived at a certain date or "always till a while ago".   The place where a non-motoring family went for holidays may be significant. Sometimes people went to relatives, or to their vicinity.   For a southern based family to holiday at Scarborough or Skegness or Yarmouth a link with the north is likely. (But Yarmouth may not be Great Yarmouth, but the one on the Isle of Wight ("The Island"). And "The Island" is Man to a Lancastrian and Canvey to an east Londoner.)

Occupations. Most people know what their fathers and siblings did. What Grandfather did may be known if they lived in the same place or holidayed with him.   Watch out for "enhancement".   If you look the sort who scorns common ancestors, then the farm labourer will become a farmer, a clerk a merchant, which could waste a lot of your time looking for him in directories where he won't appear.   If she says farmer, ask how many acres (*not* hectares)/horses/labourers, etc. – and drop the inquisition if she gets shifty.

What was he like? This is the most valuable sort of detail a really elderly person can give you. Some people will give a physical description, some a character study (or assassination). You rarely get both, so don't worrit a person who sees beneath the surface for unmemorable things like colour of hair and eyes.

Who dun it?   Victorians and Edwardians were so good at cover ups that the identity of the "real father" of a child is often shrouded in mystery. Auntie may be the only one to know, so you will have to ask her.   But get on good terms first, display your unshockability and desire for the truth. Women generally know the truth rather than men – and will often only tell another woman – men have to be protected from harsh reality.

Tracing long lost cousins

When you run out of all possible family sources, try the stranger who might belong. Finding him may involve a bit of detective work (so does genealogy).

If your name is really uncommon, then go through all the phone books for the British Isles (major reference libraries in most areas) or even for the world (some large libraries or the Guildhall, London, or major Post Offices). Extract all the addresses of the Fitzfazack-erleys and get writing (or phoning the nearer ones). You will receive a fair percentage of replies, since the less common the name, the more interest in fellow sufferers. Some may be relatives, others possibles. You then have the nucleus of a One Name Society and information on the Guild of One-Name Studies and how to run one can be obtained from *Forming a One-Name Group* (also published by the Federation, at 70p including postage from the address at the foot of the back cover).

This isn't practical with the Browns and Joneses. However, if you have located the family in one particular area not too far back, then you can try the same exercise just on the local phone book for that area, and maybe the adjacent areas. Find out which local newspaper circulates in the area from *Willing's Press Guide* (most good libraries) which will index it under the town (or nearest town) and give the address of the office. Write a letter to the Editor, setting out (briefly) what you know about the family and when your ancestor left. Give a few Christian names, occupations, local associations (he won the Bowls Trophy in 1928). Most Editors will print the letter, and there may even be a few replies. If you get something new, write to thank the Editor – he may print that. An ounce of free publicity on the editorial pages is worth a dozen small ads which no one reads.

Then visit the area. You may have contacts from the letters, but if not, collect all the relevant names from the Electoral Register (Post Office or Library). This catches the ones who aren't on the phone, or are ex-directory. It won't give you the married women, of course. Tell the girl on the desk what you are doing – she may have seen the letter and heard local people discussing it. This could lead to someone who meant to write but Jack lit the fire with the paper dear.

If the ancestors lived in a village, try the local shop, where they know everything that happened to everyone since 1893. Ask the post-man where "Arthur somebody, up by the Co-op" lives. Someone is bound to know a Mrs Thing whose maiden name was Whatsit – and that she is round the corner visiting her married daughter now.

Never be shy about contacting unknown relatives...if you are very polite and cheerfully prepared to go away and come back later, when they have had a chance to clean up a bit. Don't expect strangers to roll out the red carpet and drop everything though. Don't call at lunch time, or at night on elderly ladies living alone. The local shop may know the best time to call. Don't expect to be recognised and welcomed. People tend to reject cousins they don't know as "not belonging". Take photos, especially those connected with the place, and be prepared to tell all about yourself to prove your *bona fides*.

If your ancestors have been away more than 75 years, you may be told they were never there. Even if you contact what you are sure are relatives, they may insist they never had a great uncle Herbert and that they know nothing about the family. Leave your address and keep things friendly, and they may start digging something out for next time you are there.

"She died last week"

All too often, you track down an elderly relative, only to find that death has just beaten you to it. Tact demands that you stay away from a house of mourning. The call of family history demands that you get in there fast before all the papers are burnt. But be very, very tactful, or the bereaved will think you are after the spoons. Handled carefully, you may be a valuable source of comfort for a lonely person picking up the threads after years of caring for an invalid. You may even come away with a mass of "useless rubbish" which is pure genealogical gold. Mind that you do not upset the executor, who is custodian of all the effects.

If the old person lived alone, you may trace the next of kin through newspaper reports of the funeral, or addresses on the floral tributes on the grave. Neighbours may be able to tell you the addresses. Indeed, if the neighbours were confidantes, they may be able to tell you all about the family and know as much about your ancestors as you do. Other places to find friends of the deceased may be at the Darby and Joan Club, the W.I., the Labour or Conservative Club, the British Legion, the Bingo Club, the local pub, even the church or chapel. This copes with most of the gossiping places of the able-bodied − except the local shop.

House-bound or bedridden people may have been visited by the W.V.S. lady, a home help, a Guide or Scout or school youth club member who regularly ran errands; a hairdresser or chiropodist, the pools collector, the milkman, someone from the church, old Harry down the road or − above all − a social worker. If any of them listened to stories of the past, they may be able to repeat them for you. Social workers may have collected information about the family in an effort to contact relatives. If you appear to be the only next of kin, they may talk to you and reveal what they know. But they can turn very officious, especially if you happen to be a journalist − they are sensitive about being investigated, and may feel they could have handled the case better, had there been time.

The last person in charge of an elderly invalid often knows a great deal about the family − which is why daughters in law are often better informants than sons, out at work all day. Often grandchildren will be told more than children − there is no need to keep up a front for them. Some grandfathers are awful liars, though, and lead children astray.

Family Traditions

Every family has its traditions and, inevitably, they are not all true. They are not false either. Don't believe every word Auntie says because she looks so innocent. Maybe she is quoting Uncle Bert, who thinks he is Napoleon. Work out whether your informant was there, was adult and still remembers things. If not, what was her source? It may be Auntie Flo who was addicted to romantic novels, the aforesaid Uncle Bert, or a remark she overheard when she was four.

The tradition most likely to be true is the one that offers no advantage to the family. "Grandpa came from Wiltshire" - yes, sounds reasonable. "Grandpa was the cousin of the Earl of Mucke" - well, treat with caution. Some traditions can be proved true as soon as the official documents are checked. These are simple.

Some are true, but in a different century - great-grandpa came from Wiltshire, the five times great grandpa was cousin to Sir Henry Mucke. Some traditions are true but misunderstood. "The family used to live at Ashby Castle) - we used to live at Ashby de la Zouche (alias Ashby Castle). A child may overhear that Grandpa had "connections" with the Duke of this or the Earl of that. True. But this may turn out to be as landlord (or potman) of a pub of that name or arms. Keeping the Pig (and Whistle) becomes "hog ranching" to an emigrant grandchild.

Some traditions are misremembered. My grandmother, a lady of impeccable veracity, said her mother's maiden name was Bowman. I finally found her as Moorman. Granny said triumphantly "I knew it was something to do with a boat".

Some things were told to your informant as the truth and retailed as such. In this class come most of the stories that Great-granny was seduced by the local Squire, never the butcher, the baker or a passing tinker. Check for probability. If she was plain and 36 and the Squire had a string of glamorous mistresses, probably not. If she was young, very pretty, worked at the manor and the local paper says he was at home at the relevant time, well, maybe. If the child in question is the image of the ffoulenough ancestors, rather than of the bootboy she married three months later, well, even more maybe. If she was given a huge dowry and the child was later educated beyond his station, well, very likely. Don't believe everything you are told - but don't ignore it either.

The Documents in the Case

Every family has about its collective person some useful documents. Apart from birth, marriage and death certificates, wills, and insurance policies, which you may be allowed to see and copy details from, there are other things to ask for. Memorial cards and funeral certificates; grave space receipts; Granny's birthday book, with all the family names in it; school and Sunday school reports and prizes; apprenticeship indentures; army Rolls of Honour (death date, rank and regiment); samplers (name, age and date); birthday present books, photos (mentioned earlier); sports and hobby trophies; holiday souvenirs (a Present from Clacton); army or navy mementoes (regiment, ship?); souvenirs of the British Raj (who served in India?) and receipts, which are kept for an incredible time and give addresses and some idea of life style. And there might even be a family bible.

You should never turn down anything as trivial or useless. Gain a family reputation as a home for any old rubbish - and one day it will pay off.

Remember

It isn't necessarily true because Auntie Maggie said it.
It isn't necessarily a lie because Uncle Bert said it.
If none of the names check at St. Catherine's, try a different year. If there is still no sign, are you looking for pet names?
Polly (or Molly) is Mary Ann (or Mary).
Tillie or Mattie is Matilda.
Nellie is Ellen or Eleanor or Helen.
Patty (or Matty) is Martha, not Patricia till 1920 plus.
Peggy or Meg or Maggie or Molly is Margaret - so is Greta sometimes.
Jenny or Jinny is Jane or Jean or Joan or Janet.
Fred is Frederick or Alfred.
Bert is Albert or Herbert or Robert - Bertie is Bertram.
Lal is Lawrence or Albert; Loll, Lowry, Larry is Lawrence.
Bessie, Lizzie, Libby, Betty, Beth, Liza is Elizabeth (or Eliza).
Nora (might be Eleanora, Honora).
Nancy is Ann.
Dolly is Dorothy - so is Dora, sometimes.
Cissie might be Cicely but is usually = Sister, so could be anything.
Nip(per), Kid(da) - general term for younger brother.

The Written Questionnaire

If you must write, because you are tied to the house or the relative is overseas, you will have to explain what you are after and give information about yourself and your immediate forebears. Then you have a choice. You can say vaguely, "Tell me all about your family", or send a questionnaire with very detailed requests and a space for the answer to be filled in. The first risks getting "I am a widow and have no family left over here". The second risks being thrown in the bin as impertinent nosiness. Possibly a combination of both is the best you can do. Some people will junk the form and write a letter, some will fill in some of the form, some, bless them, will do both. Some won't answer at all. But usually people overseas are keener to know of links with home than people who live in Britain.

A sample for one person is:

Your father's name ....

His date of birth .... Where born ....

His school(s) .... (dates)

His career (jobs in order) .... (2-3 lines)

Was he in the army/navy/airforce ....

Regiment, ship, squadron ....

Where did he serve ....

Where did he live .... (please give dates)

.... (3-4 lines)

Date of death .... Where ....

Where buried ....

Date of marriage .... Where ....

(similar details of your mother)
(list and dates of children).

Repeat this for everyone you think might be known — stating very clearly "your father's father", "your mother's father" not "grandfather".

If you want information about all the brothers and sisters and their families, you will have to provide a lot of sheets of paper, and this is going to cost rather a lot to post. Sent airmail overseas you will reach 50p in no time — so select carefully before you commit yourself to writing to every single person of the name. It is polite to send an S.A.E. inland or two International Reply Coupons (from the Post Office) overseas, so this is going to cost you a fair bit. You could try a general appeal through the various family history societies in the countries involved.